Pagan Origins

of the

Christ Myth

John G. Jackson

ISBN 978-1-60386-732-0

Contents

Part One:

Pagan Origins *of the* Christ Myth

T he cardinal doctrines of the Christian religion are (1) the Fall of Man and (2) the Atonement. There are liberal Christian apologists who no longer subscribe to a literal belief in the Fall of Man. They have relegated Adam and Eve to the realm of Mythology. These liberals are opposed by orthodox apologists, who declare that belief in the Atonement implies belief in the Fall of Man. Logic seems to be on the orthodox side. As T. W. Doane has pointed out:

> These two dogmas cannot be separated from each other. *If there was no Fall, there is no need of an atonement, and no Redeemer is required.* Those, then, who consent in recognizing in Christ Jesus a God and Redeemer, and who, notwithstanding, cannot resolve upon admitting the story of the Fall of Man to be *historical*, should exculpate themselves from the reproach of *inconsistency*.[1]

Anyone who is familiar with the elements of the higher criticism knows that there are two stories of the Creation and Fall of Man in the book of Genesis. The first, or Priestly Account, was written in the fifth century B.C. and extends from the beginning of Genesis through verse 3 of chapter 2. The second, or Jehovistic Account, begins with verse 4 of chapter 2, and extends through the third chapter. This version of the story was written in the eight century B.C. It is

---

[1] T. W. Doane, *Bible Myths and Their Parallels in Other Religions, Being a Comparison of the Old and New Testament Myths and Miracles with Those of Heathen Nations of Antiquity Considering also Their Origin and Meaning* (New York: The Truth Seeker Company, 1882), p. 17.

interesting to note that the second narrative is about three hundred years older than the first. In the following comparison of these two tales, the Priestly version is designated by the letter P, and the Jehovistic version by the letters J.E. These documents differ in six important points, to wit:

1. P: The earth emerges from the waters. It is saturated with moisture.

J.E.: The world is at first a dry plain. There was no vegetation, because "the Lord God had not caused it to rain upon the earth."[2]

2. P: Birds and beasts are created before man. J.E.: Man is created before the birds and beasts.

3. P: All fowls that fly are made out of the waters. J.E.: The Fowls of the air are made out of the ground.

4. P: Man is created in the image of god.

J.E.: Man is made out of the dust of the ground. It is only after eating of the forbidden fruit that god said, "Behold, the man is become as one of us."[3]

5. P.: Man is made lord of the whole earth.

J.E: Man is merely placed in the garden to dress it and keep it.

6. P.: Man and woman are created together, as the closing and completing work of the whole creation.

J.E.: Man is created first, then beasts and birds are, which are named by man. Finally, the woman is made out of a rib of the man.

Orthodox Christians claim that both of these stories must be believed, even though they contradict each other at numerous points. There have been eminent Christian authorities,

---

[2] Genesis 2:5
[3] Genesis 3:22.

however, who have rejected a literal view of Genesis. The celebrated Church father, Bishop Origen wrote as follows:

> What man of sense will agree with the statement that the first, second and third days, in which the evening is named and the morning, were without sun, moon and stars? What man is found such an idiot as to suppose that God planted trees in Paradise like a husbandman? I believe every man must hold these things for images under which a hidden sense is concealed.[4]

St. Augustine[5] declared that "There is no way of preserving the first chapter of Genesis without impiety, and attributing things to God unworthy of Him." There is, of course, nothing unique about these Hebraic Eden myths. They were known among the so-called heathens thousands of years before the Bible was invented. Two very fine examples are cited by Sir Godfrey Higgins, the English orientalist, as follows:

1. "Another striding instance is recorded by the very intelligent traveler (Wilson) regarding a representation of the fall of our first parents, sculptured in the magnificent temple of Ipsambul in Nubia. He says that a very exact representation of Adam and Eve in the Garden of Eden is to be seen in that cave, and that the serpent climbing round the tree is especially delineated, and the whole subject of the tempting of our first parents most accurately exhibited."[6]

2. "A drawing, brought by Colonel Coombs, from a sculptured column in a cave- temple in the South of India, represents the first pair at the foot of the ambrosial tree, and a

---

[4] Origen (A.D. 185?-254?), Greek writer, teacher and church father. *On First Principles*, trans. G. W. Butterworth (Magnolia, MA: Peter Smith)

[5] St. Augustine (353-430), church father, bishop of Hippo (396-430), The Confessions of St. Augustine and City of God (New York: Dorset Books, 1961)

[6] Godfrey Higgins, Esq., *Anacalypsis: An Attempt to Draw Aside the Veil of the Saitic Isis; or an Inquiry into the Origin of Languages, Nations and Religions*, 2 vols, (new York: J. W. Bouton, 1878), vol. 1, p.403.

serpent entwined among the heavily-laden boughs, presenting to them some of the fruit from his mouth."[7]

Mr. George Smith, of the Department of Oriental Antiquity of the British Museum, discovered Assyrian terra-cotta tablets in the ruins of Nineveh, dating from 1500 to 2000 B.C., which give not only the story of the creation of Man, but narratives of the Deluge and the Tower of Babel as well. In referring to an engraving on an Assyrian cylinder, Mr. Smith notes that:

> *One striking and important specimen of early type in the British Museum collection has two figures sitting one on each side of a tree, holding out their hands to the fruit, while at the back of one (the woman) is scratched a serpent . . . thus it is evident that a form of the Fall, similar to that of Genesis, was known in early times in Babylonia.*[8]

In the original Babylonian Eden myth, as translated from a Sumerian tablet by Professor Edward Chiera, there is the story of a great conflict among the gods. They cannot decide whether man ought to be created or not. A wise old reptile, the dragon Tiamat, opposed the creation of the human race. The dragon fought against the great god Bel. Finally the god overcame the dragon by blasting him with thunderbolts. Opposition having been crushed, man was created. This conflict between Bel and the dragon bears a close analogy to the story of the Revolution in Heaven recorded in the Apocalypse:

> *And there was war in heaven: Michael and his angels fought against the dragon; and the dragon fought and his angels.*
>
> *And prevailed not; neither was their place found any more in heaven.*

---

[7] Higgins, *Anacalypsis*, vol. 1, pp. 403–404.

[8] George Smith, *The Chaldean Account of Genesis* (New York: 1876), p. 91.

And the great dragon was cast out, that old serpent, called the Devil, and Satan, which deceiveth the whole world: he was cast out into the earth, and his angels were cast out with him.[9]

The myths of the Fall are based on man's yearning for immortality. Due to the habit of certain species of snakes periodically shedding their skins, primitive man got the idea that serpents were immortal. The natural vanity of man told our distant ancestors that the gods had intended the gift of eternal life for humanity alone. So it was conceived that the serpent had stolen the precious prize from the human race. The biblical version of the Fall of Man is incomplete. The role of the serpent in not explained, and the Tree of Life is not given due prominence in the story. The original story, which we are able to piece together from fragments gathered from the mythology of many lands, reads as follows:

God placed the first man and woman in a garden of delights. In this garden were two trees, the Tree of Life and the Tree of Death (called the Tree of Knowledge in the Bible). Man had the choice of eating the fruit of the Tree of life and becoming immortal, or of eating the fruit of the Tree of Death and becoming mortal. God sent the serpent to tell Adam and Eve to eat of the fruit of the Tree of Life, so that they might live forever, and to warn them against eating of the fruit of the Tree of Death, for if they should eat this forbidden fruit they would surely die, and this course would descend to their children from generation to generation. The wily serpent, however, reversed the message. He told the first human pair that they would obtain immortality by eating of the fruit of the Tree of Death. Unfortunately Adam and Eve believed the diabolical snake, ate the forbidden fruit, and as a consequence were expelled from Eden and became mortal. The sly

---

[9] Revelations 12:7-9.

reptile, on the other hand, helped himself to the fruit of the Tree of Life and gained immortal life for himself and his kind.

For a masterly study of myths concerning the Fall of Man, the reader is referred to volume 1 of Sir James George Frazer's *Folk-Lore in the Old Testament*.[10] Frazer holds that the Hebrews got their version, directly or indirectly from Africa:

> Even if the story should hereafter be found in a Sumerian version this would not absolutely exclude the hypothesis of its African origin, since the original home of the Sumerians is unknown. ... In favor of the African origin of the myth it may be observed that the explanation of the supposed immortality of serpents, which probably furnished the kernel of the story in its original form, has been preserved in several African versions, while it has been wholly lost in the Hebrew version; from which it is natural to infer that the African versions are older and nearer to the original than the corresponding but incomplete narratives in Genesis.[11]

The hypothetical first man of the Bible is rightly named Adam, since the word Adam, which means "Man," was reputedly made out of *Adamah*, which means the "Ground" or "Earth." Similarly among the ancient Romans, man was called *Homo*, because he was supposedly made from *Humus*, the Earth. According to an ancient Egyptian myth, Knoumou, the father of the gods, molded the earliest men out of clay on a potter's wheel. We are informed by the Chaldean priest, Berosus, that the great god Bel decapitated himself, and that the other gods mixed his blood with clay, and out of it

---

[10] Sir James George Frazer, *Folk-Lore in the Old Testament: Studies in Comparative Religion, Legend, and Law*, 3 vols. (London: Macmillan and Co., Limited, 1918).

[11] Sir James George Frazer, *Worship of Nature*, Gifford Lectures 1924-25 (1926), P. 223-244

fashioned the first man. In the Greek mythology, Prometheus is depicted as manufacturing men from clay at Panopeus.[12]

---

[12] For scholarly studies of these creation tales the curious reader is referred to *Folk-Lore in the Old Testament*, by Sir J. G. Frazer, and *Forgery in Christianity: A Documented Record of the Foundations of the Christian Religion*, by Major Joseph Wheless (Moscow, Idaho: "Psychiana," 1930).

Part Two:

The Christ Myth

T he triumph of the doctrine of evolution has reconciled the more literate Christians to the non-historicity of Adam. As the historicity of Jesus, however, is now widely questioned, even the most liberal defenders of the faith find themselves in a very uncomfortable position, being belabored by both fundamentalists and ultra-rationalists alike. After surrendering the theological Christ, the liberal Christian apologist finds out, much to his chagrin, that practically nothing is known about the historical Jesus. Our chief sources of information concerning Jesus Christ are the so-called genuine Pauline Epistles and references to Jesus by Jewish and pagan writers, but most of these are of extremely doubtful authenticity.

There is a famous passage in *The Antiquities of the Jews*, by Flavius Jesephus,[13] in which reference is made to Jesus Christ, but it is generally regarded as a forgery, even by Christian scholars. The passage is not mentioned by any Christian writer before Eusebius, in the early part of the fourth century.

Cornelius Tacitus, the Roman historian, in his celebrated *Annals*,[14] refers to the burning of Rome in 64 A.D. and the Neroian persecution of the Christians. He describes them as a "vast multitude" and says that the cult was founded by

---

[13] Flavius Josephus (ca A.D. 37-A.D. 100), Jewish historian, *The Works of Flavins Josephus: Comprising the Antiquities of he Jews; A History of the Jewish Wars; and Life of Flavius Josephus*, written by himself, 2 vols. Trans. William Whiston (Philadelphia: Jas. B. Smith & Co., 1859).

[14] Cornelius Tacitus (ca 56 — ca 120), Roman historians *Annals*, trans. Arthur Murphy (London; Jones & Co., 1830).

Christus, who was punished as a criminal by the Procurator Pontius Pilate. Eusebius[15] made a list of Jewish and pagan references to Christianity, but Tactus is not mentioned by him. In fact, the passage in question was not quoted by any Christian writer before the fifteenth century. Pliny the younger, proconsul of Bithynia, wrote a letter to the Roman Emperor Tragan (early second century), in which he reported the presence in his province of a group of people who gathered before daybreak on a certain day and sang hymns to Christ as a god. There is no evidence that this Christ was the Jesus of the Gospels. The Emperor Hadrian in a letter to the Consul Servianus (A.D. 134), asserts that the worshippers of the sun-god Serapis, in Egypt, were Christians, and that these sun-worshippers called themselves "Bishops of Christ." The worship of Serapis was imported into Egypt from Pontus, a province bordering on Bithynia. The Christians mentioned by Pliny the Younger[16] were in all probability worshippers of Serapis.

Suetonius[17] in his "Life of Claudius" relates that "He (Claudius) drove the Jews, who at the instigation of Christas were constantly rioting, out of Rome." This is said to have taken place about fifteen years after the crucifixion of Jesus. So Chistas could hardly have been Jesus Christ. Philo, an eminent Jewish philosopher and historian, was a contemporary of Christ, but makes no mention of Jesus. Philo developed the doctrine of the Logos, and although according to Christian theology Jesus Christ was the Logos, he was not aware of the

---

[15] Eusebius (ca 260 — ca 339), theologian and church historian, bishop of Caesarea, *Ecclesiastical History*, trans. C. F. Cruse (London: George Bell & Sons, 1874).

[16] Gaius Plinius Caecilius Secundus [Pliny the] Younger (A.D. 61 [or 62]-ca A.D. 113) "Letters to the Emperor Trajan," *Letters of The Younger Pliny*, 2 vols. (1978 reprint; Philadelphia: R. West).

[17] G. Suetonius Tranquillus (ca A.D. 69-after 122), Roman biographer and historian, *Lives of the First Caesars* (reprint 1976; New York: AMS Press, 1970).

identity. Justus of Tiberias, a native of Galilee, wrote a history covering the period in which Justus is said to have lived, but does not in any instance call the name of the Christ. The works of Justus have now all perished, but they were read by Photius, a Christian bishop and scholar, of Constantinople (ninth century). Says Photius: "He (Justus) makes not the least mention of the appearance of Christ, of what things happened to him, or of the wonderful work that he did.[18] The paucity of our information concerning the Christian savior is concisely expressed by Mr. Robert Keable, in his work, *The Great Galilean*:

> No man knows sufficient of the early life of Jesus to write a biography of him. For that matter, no one knows enough for the normal *Times* obituary notice of a great man. If regard were had to what we should call, in correct speech, definitely historical facts, scarcely three lines could be filled. Moreover, if newspapers had been in existence, and if that obituary notice had had to be written in the year of his death, no editor could have found in the literature of his day so much as his name. Yet few periods of the ancient world were so well documented as the period of Augustus and Tiberius. But no contemporary knew of his existence. Even a generation later, a spurious passage in Josephus, a questionable reference in Suetonius, and the mention of a name that may be his by Tacitus—that is all. His first mention in any surviving document, secular or religious, is twenty years after.

The so-called genuine Pauline Epistles, in the New Testament, are Romans, 1 and 2 Corinthians, and Galatians. The other letters attributed to St. Paul are regarded as spurious. The genuine Epistles were written from about A.D. 52 to 64.

---

[18] Photius (ca 820-891), patriarch of Constantinople (858-876 and 878-886), *Codices*.

The dates of origin of the Four Gospels have been estimated as follows: Mark—A.D. 70 to 100; Luke—about A.D. 100; Matthew—A.D. 100 to 1 10; John—sometime between A.D. 100 and 160. That these Gospels stories are replete with inaccuracies and contradictions is obvious to all who read with a discerning eye. In Mathew 2:1, we are told that Jesus Christ was born "in the days of Herod." But in Luke 2:2, were are told that the Christ child first saw the light of day, "when Cyrenious was governor of Syria." There is here a discrepancy of at least ten years, for Herod died in the year 4. B.C. while Cyrenius, or Quirinius, as he is known in Roman history, did not become governor of Syria until the year A.D. 7. According to the Rev. Dr. Giles, in his *Hebrew and Christian Records*: "We have no clue to either the day or the time of year, or even the year itself, in which Christ was born." Matthew 1:6-16 lists twenty-eight generations from David to Jesus while Luke 3:23-38 tabulates forty-three. According to John, Jesus visited Jerusalem at least four times, but the Synoptics (Mark, Luke and Matthew) assure us that he journeyed to that city only once. As to the length of the Jesus' ministry the Synoptics say one year, but John says at least three years. From the Synoptical account, we gather that the savior carried out his work chiefly in Galilee, but John informs us that Judea was the principal theater of the ministry of Christ.

The hour of the crucifixion is likewise uncertain. One account fixes the time at the third hour (9 A.M.).[19] Another account says it occurred at about the sixth hour (Noon).[20] It is alleged that Jesus predicted that he would sojourn in the tomb for three days and three nights.[21] But in the Synoptic accounts of the event, as it is said to have actually happened, the time is given as two nights and one day, *i.e.*, one day and a half.

---

[19] Mark 15:25.
[20] 8. Luke 23:44.
[21] Matthew 12:40.

Should we inquire as to who visited the tomb first, we receive four different answers. John says one woman; Mathew, two women; Mark, three women; and Luke, a crowd of women. When we ask whom did the women meet at the tomb, we again receive four replies. Matthew asserts that they saw one angel, whereas Mark declares it was one young man. According to Luke, the women saw two men. And John says that they saw two angels. These women also saw Jesus, if we believe Matthew (chapter 28). If we give credence to Luke (chapter 24), the women did not see Jesus.

Nor do these inspired scribes display unanimity regarding the number of days between the resurrection and the ascension. The elapsed time was only one day, if we follow Luke, and at least ten days if we take the work of John. The Book of Acts extends the period to forty days. Since both the Gospel according to Luke and the Book of Acts are said to have been written by the Author, these discrepancies are very puzzling, to say the least. According to Holy Writ, Jesus the Christ terminated his earthy pilgrimage by ascending to heaven. The exact location of his departure, it seems, it unknown. The ascension took place in Jerusalem, if Mark wrote correctly. Not so, if Luke knew whereof he spoke, for he relates that it was at Bethany. Acts (1:12) gives Mt. Olivet as the scene of the momentous event. Let it be noted that Matthew and John make no mention of the ascension; that it occurs in Mark in the Spurious Addendum (the last twelve verses, which were not in the original manuscript), and that Luke's version does not appear in the *Codes Sinaiticus*, a fourth-century manuscript now in the British Museum. The Gospel writers advance three views as to the nature of Jesus. Mark regards him as the Son of Man. Matthew and Luke hail him as the Son of God, while John recognizes him as God himself.

A consideration of pagan parallels will put the Gospel records in a clearer light. Let us become as little children, and travel backwards in time, with a venerable bishop as our guide:

Suppose you had been a child living in Rome 1940 years ago; that is, a few years before Jesus is supposed to have been born. About a week before December twenty-fifth, you could have found everybody preparing for a great feast, just as they do in Europe today. To those Romans December twenty-fifth was the birthday of the sun. They wrote that in gold letters in their calendar. Every year about that time, the middle of winter, the sun was born once more and it was going to put an end to the darkness and misery of winter. So they had a great feast, with presents and dolls for everybody, and the best day of all was December twenty-fifth. That feast, they would tell you, was thousands of years old—before Christ was ever heard of...

Just outside Rome there was an underground temple of the Persian God Mithra. Well, at midnight, the first minute of December twenty-fifth, you would have seen that temple all lit up with candles, and priests in white garments at the altar, and boys burning incense; exactly as you will see in a Roman Catholic church at midnight on December twenty-fourth in our own time. And the worshippers of Mithra would have told you that Mithra was a good God who had come from heaven to be born as a man and redeem men from their sins; and he was born in a dark cave or stable on December twenty-fifth.

Then suppose you asked somebody where the Egyptians who lived in Rome had their temple. You would have found these also celebrating the birth of their savior-god Horus who was born of a virgin in a stable on December twenty-fifth. In the temple you would find a statue of figure of the infant-god Horus lying in a manger, and a statue of his virgin-mother Isis standing beside it; just as in a Roman Catholic church on Christmas day you will find a stable or cave rigged up and the infant Jesus in a manger and a figure of Mary beside it.

Then you might go to the Greek temple, and find them paying respect to the figure of their savior-god in a manger or cradle. And if you found the quarters of the gladiators, the war-captives from Germany, you would have found these also holding a feast, and they would explain that December twenty-fifth (or mid-winter) was, all over Europe, the great feast of Yule, or the Wheel, which means that the sun had turned back, like a wheel, and was going once more to redeem men from the hell of winter to the heaven of summer.[22]

---

[22] Bishop William Montgomery Brown, *Science and History for Girls and Boys* (Gallon, OH: The Bradford-Brown Educational Company, 1932), pp. 138-139.

Part Three:

Pagan Christs

T he Egyptian analogies to the Christian epic are so close in some cases as to suggest an Egyptian origin for certain Christian doctrines and rites. This is clearly shown by Gerald Massey:

> The Christian dispensation is believed to have been ushered in by the birth of a child, and the portrait of that child in the Roman Catacombs as the child of Mary is the youthful Sun-God in the Mummy Image of the child- king, the Egyptian Karast, or Christ. The alleged facts of our Lord's life as Jesus the Christ, were equally the alleged facts of our Lord's life as the Horus of Egypt, whose very name signifies the Lord. . . . The Jesus Christ with female paps, who is the Alpha and Omega of Revelation, was the Iu of Egypt, and Iao of the Chaldeans. Jesus as the Lamb of God, and Ichthys the Fish, was Egyptian. Jesus as the Coming One; Jesus born of the Virgin Mother, who was overshadowed by the Holy Ghost, Jesus born of two mothers, both of whose names are Mary; Jesus born in the manger—at Christmas, and again at Easter; Jesus saluted by the three kings, or Magi; Jesus of the transfiguration on the Mount; Jesus whose symbol in the Catacombs is the eight-rayed Star—the Star of the East; Jesus as the eternal Child; Jesus as God the Father, re-born as his own Son; Jesus as the child of twelve years; Jesus as the Anointed One of thirty years; Jesus in his Baptism; Jesus walking on the Waters, or working his Miracles; Jesus as the Caster-out of demons; Jesus as a Substitute, who suffered in a

vicarious atonement for sinful men; Jesus whose followers are the two brethren, the four fishers, the seven fishers, the twelve apostles, the seventy (or seventy-two in some texts) whose names were written in Heaven; Jesus who was administered to by seven women; Jesus in his bloody sweat; Jesus betrayed by Judas; Jesus as Conqueror of the grave; Jesus the Resurrection and the Life; Jesus before Herod; in the Hades, and in his re-appearance to the women and to the seven fishers; Jesus who was crucified both on the 14* and 15* of the month Nisan; Jesus who was also crucified in Egypt (as it is written in Revelation); Jesus as judge of the Dead, with the sheep on the right, and the goats on the left, is Egyptian from first to last, in every phase from the beginning to the end.[23]

Osiris,[24] the father of Horus, was another virgin-born god of ancient Egypt. His Sufferings, Death, and Resurrection were celebrated in an annual mystery-play at Abydos, on about March 25, an approximation of the Vernal Equinox, i.e. Easter. The Pharaoh Amenhotep III, of the seventeenth dynasty, was hailed as the son of the virgin Mutemua. His birth is pictured on the inner walls of the Temple of Amen in Thebes. "In this picture," declares the Egyptologist Samuel Sharpe,

---

[23] Gerald Massey, *The Historical Jesus and the Mythical Christ or Natural Genesis and Typology of Equinoctial Chistolatry* (London: 1936), pp. 42-43. For an exhaustive treatment, see Massey's book *A Book of the Beginnings Containing an Attempt to Recover and Reconstitute the Lost Origins* [sic] *of the Myths and Mysteries, Types and Symbols, Religion and Language, with Egypt for the Mouthpiece and Africa as the Birthplace*, 2 vols. (Secaucas, NJ: University Books Inc., 1974). Other valuable references are Samuel Sharpe's *Egyptian Mythology*; James Bonwick's *Egyptian Belief and Modern Thought*; James G. Frazer's Adonis, Attis, *Osiris Studies in the History of Oriental Religion*, 3 ed., (New York: St. Martin, 1976); and T. W. Doane's *Bible Myths*.

[24] Osiris was the great Egyptian god of the underworld and the judge of the dead.

We have the Annunciation, the Conception, the Birth
and the Adoration, as described in the first and second
chapters of Luke's gospel; and as we have historical
assurance that the chapters in Matthew's gospel which
contain the miraculous birth are an after addition not in
the earliest manuscripts, it seems probable that these
two poetical chapters in Luke may also be unhistorical,
and borrowed from the Egyptian accounts of the
miraculous births of their kings.

Another great pagan christ was Krishna[25] of India. In the
sacred books of India it is recorded that Krishna was born of
the virgin Devaki, that his nativity was heralded by a star,
and that though of royal lineage, he was born in a cave.
(According to the apocryphal gospel of Protevagelion,[26] a work
attributed to James, the brother of Jesus, the Christian savior
was born in a cave.) At the time of Krishna's birth, the cave
was mysteriously illuminated. (At the birth of Jesus, "there
was a great light in the cave, so that the eyes of Joseph and the
Midwife could not bear it.") The infant Krishna spoke to his
mother soon after his birth. ("Jesus spake even when he was in
the cradle, and said to his mother: 'Mary I am Jesus the Son of
God, that Word which thou did bring forth according to the
declaration of the Angel Gabriel unto thee, and my Father
hath sent me for the salvation of the world'[27] according to the
apocryphal gospels of 1 and 2 Infancy.) Krishna was born
while his foster-father Nanda was in the city to pay his tax to
the king. (Jesus was born while his foster-father Joseph was in
the city to pay his tax to the governor.[28]) The babe Krishna

---

[25] Krishna was the eighth avatar (incarnation) of Vishnu and one of the
most widely worshipped of the Hindu gods.
[26] Protevagelion in *The Apocryphal New Testament, being all the Gospels,
Epistles, and Other Pieces now Extant, Attributed in the First Four Centuries
to Jesus Christ, His Apostles, and Their Companions, and not Included in The
New Testament by its Compilers* (New York: Peter Eckler Publishing Co.,
1927).
[27] 1 and 2 Infancy in *The Apocryphal New Testament.*
[28] Luke 2:1-3, 5

was adored by cowherds. (The infant Jesus was adored by shepherds.) King Kansa sought the life of the Indian Christ by ordering the massacre of all male children born during the same night as was Krishna. (This is almost identical with the story of the slaughter of the innocents, ordered by Herod.[29]) Nanda was warned by a heavenly voice to flee with the infant Khrisna across the Jumna River, to Gakul, to escape King Kansa. (Joseph was warned by a voice in a dream to flee into Egypt with the Christ-child to escape the wrath of Herod.) Krishna performed many miracles in the city of Mathura. (Jesus, while in Egypt, lived in a town named Matarea, where he performed many miracles.) Krishna was a crucified christ. He is pictured in Indian art as hanging on a cross with arms extended. (Dr. Thomas Inman, a celebrated authority on pagan and Christian symbolism, states that: "Christna, whose history so closely resembles our Lord's, was also like him in his being crucified."[30]) Krishna was pierced by an arrow while hanging on the cross. (Jesus was pierced by a spear during his crucifixion.) The light of the sun was blotted out at noon on the day of Krishna's death. (The sun was darkened from the sixth to the ninth hour on the day of the crucifixion of Christ.) Krishna descended into hell to raise the dead before returning to the abode of the gods. (We read of Jesus Christ that: "He descended into hell and on the third day rose again from the dead." The Descent into Hell of Jesus is described in the apocryphal gospel of Nicodemus.[31]) Krishna rose from the grave, and finally ascended bodily to heaven in the presence of a multitude of spectators. (A similar story is related of Jesus Christ.) In Indian art Krishna literally means "The Black." (In early Christian art Jesus is almost invariably represented as a Black man.) Sir Godfrey Higgins made a thorough

---

[29] According to Matthew 2:16.

[30] Thomas Inman, M.D., *Ancient Faiths Embodied in Ancient Names*, vol. 1 p. 441 ; cited by T. W. Doane in *Bible Myths*, p. 186.

[31] Nicodemus in *The Apocryphal New Testament*.

investigation of the pictures and images of Black Infants and Madonnas in the cathedrals of Europe.

"[I]n all the Romish countries of Europe," says he, "in France, Italy, Germany *etc.*, the God Christ, as well as his mother, are described in their old pictures and statues to be black. The infant God in the arms of his black mother, his eyes and drapery white, is himself perfectly black. If the reader doubt my word, he may go to the cathedral at Moulins—to the famous chapel of the Virgin at Loretto—to the church of the Annunciata—the church of St. Lazaro, or the church of St. Stephen at Genoa—to St. Francisco at Pisa—to the church at Brixen, in the Trol, and to that at Padua—to the church of St. Theodore, at Munich, in the two last of which the whiteness of the eyes and teeth, and the studied redness of the lips, are very observable;—to a church and to the cathedral at Augsburg, where are a black virgin and child as large as life: to Rome, and the Borghese chapel Maria Maggiore—to the Pantheon—to a small chapel of St. Peter's, on the right-hand side on entering, near the door; and, in fact, to almost innumerable other churches, in countries professing the Romish religion.

There is scarcely an old church in Italy where some remains of the worship of the **BLACK VIRGIN** and **BLACK** child are not to be met with. Very often the black figures have given way to white ones, and in these cases the black ones, as being held sacred, were put into retired places in the churches, but were not destroyed, and are yet to be found there. . . .

When the circumstance has been named to the Romish priests, they have endeavored to disguise the fact, by pretending that the child had become black by the smoke of the candles; but it was black where the smoke of the candle never came: and, besides, how came the candles not to blacken the white of the eyes, the teeth, and the shirt, and how came they to redden the lips? . . . Their real blackness in not to be questioned for a moment. . . .

A black virgin and child among the white Germans, Swiss, French and Italians!!![32]

Krishna was the second person in the Hindu Trinity, which consisted of: (I) Brahma, (2) Vishnu and (3) Siva. Krishna was the human incarnation of Vishnu. (Jesus Christ is considered to be the second person in the Christian Trinity.)

The close parallels between the life-stories of Buddha and Christ are just as remarkable as those between Krishna and Christ. Buddha[33] was born of a virgin name Maya, or Mary. His birthday was celebrated on December 25. He was visited by wise men who acknowledged his divinity. The life of Buddha was sought by King Bimbasara, who feared that someday the child would endanger his throne. At the age of twelve, Buddha excelled the learned men of the temple in knowledge and wisdom. His ancestry was traced back to Maha Sammata, the first monarch in the world. (Jesus' ancestry is traced back to Adam, the first man in the world.) Buddha was transfigured on a mountain top. His form was illumined by as aura of bright light. (Jesus was likewise transfigured on a mountain top. "And his face did shine as the sun, and his raiment was white as the light."[34] After the completion of his earthly mission, Buddha ascended bodily to the celestial realms.

---

[32] Higgins, *Anacalypsos*, vol. 1, pp. 138-139.

[33] Buddha is said to have been a mortal sage, whose name was Siddhartha Gautama (563-483 B.C). He was surnamed Buddha, "the awakened (enlightned)."

[34] Matthew 17:2.

Mithra,[35] a Persian sun-god, was virgin -born, in a cave, on December 25. His earliest worshippers were shepherds, and he was accompanied in his travels by twelve companions. The Mithraists kept the sabbath day holy and celebrated the Eucharist by eating wafers embellished with a cross. The great Mithraic festivals were the Birth (Christmas) and the Resurrection (Easter).

Adonis[36] or Tammuz of Babylonia was also born of a virgin. He died a cruel death, descended into hell, arose from the tomb and ascended to heaven. In a mid-summer festival, the worshippers of Adonis wept over an effigy of the dead god which was washed with water, anointed day the Resurrection was re-enacted, after which the crowd shouted: "The Lord is Risen." Finally his ascension was simulated in the presence of his devotees.

Attis[37] of Phrygia was called the Good Shepherd, and was said to be the son of the virgin Nana. It is reported that Attis, when in his prime, mutilated himself and bled to death under a sacred pine tree. The Festivals of the Death and Resurrection of Attis were staged by his worshippers from March 22 through March 25. A pine tree was cut on March 22, and an image of the god was tied to the trunk. He was shown as "slain and hanged on a tree."[38] Then the effigy was buried in a tomb. On the night of March 24, the priests opened the tomb and found it empty. The Resurrection of Attis was celebrated on March 25. His followers were baptized in blood, thereby having their sins washed away, and they were therefore declared to have been "born again."

---

[35] Mithra was a fifth century B.C. Persian god of light, who aided in the struggle with the powers of darkness.

[36] Adonis, a classical Greek mythology, a youth of remarkable beauty, a favorite of the goddess Aphrodite, symbolizing the cycle of growing seasons.

[37] Attis (Atys), a deity worshipped in Phrygia, and later throughout the Roman empire, in conjunction with the Great Mother of the Gods.

[38] Cf. New Testament: Acts 5:30.

Strange as it may seem, the Aztecs of ancient Mexico likewise could boast of a crucified savior. Quetzalcoatl[39] was born of a virgin, and also, like Jesus, was tempted and fasted for forty days. He is shown in the Borgian Ms., on a cross, with nail marks on his hands and feet. He is depicted as a man of sable hue. After being crucified, he rose from the dead and went into the East. The Mexicans were expecting his Second Coming when the Spaniards invaded the country in the sixteenth century.

---

[39] Quetzalcoatl (Feathered Serpent), a great Toltec deity, a god of the air, and in legend a saintly ruler and civilizer.

Part Four:

Sources *of the* Christ Myth

T here are two principal types of savior-gods recognized by hierologists, namely: vegetation-gods and sungods. The vegetation theory has been brilliantly developed by Sir James George Frazer, in his *Golden* Bough,[40] and by Grant Allen in The Evolution of the *Idea of God*.[41] This viewpoint is concisely summarized by the noted psychologist Dr. David Forsyth:

> Many gods besides Christ have been supposed to die, be resurrected and ascend to heaven. This idea has now been traced back to its origin among primitive people in the annual death and resurrection of crops and plant life generally. This explains the world-wide prevalence of the notion. Among still more primitive tribes, as Grant Allen showed, it is not yet understood that sown corn sprouts because of the spring sunshine, and they attribute the result to divine agency. To this end they are accustomed at seed time to kill their tribal god— either in human or animal form—and scatter the flesh and the blood over the sown fields. They believe that the seeds will not grow unless the god is sacrificed and added to them in this manner. When, therefore, the crops appears, they never doubt that it is their god coming to life again. It is from this erroneous belief of

---

[40] Sir James George Frazer, *The Golden Bough: A Study in Magic and Religion*, 13 vols. (London: Macmillan Company, 1951).
[41] Grant Allen, *The Evolution of the Idea of God: An Inquiry into the Origins of Religion* (New York: Henry Holt and Company, 1897).

primitive tribes that Christianity today derives its belief in Christ's Death and Resurrection.[42]

According to the advocates of the solar myth theory, the ancient crucified saviors were personifications of the sun, and their life-stories were allegories of the sun's passage through the twelve constellations of the Zodiac.[43] The astronomical elements in the Christian Epic are pointed out by Edward Carpenter with characteristic lucidity:

> The Passover, the greatest feast of the Jews, borrowed from the Egyptians, handed down to become the supreme festival of Christianity, ... is, as well known, closely connected with the celebration of the Spring Equinox and the passing over of the Sun from south to north of the equator, *i.e.*, from his winter depression to his summer dominion. The Sun, at the moment of passing the equinoctial point, stood three thousand years ago in the Zodiacal constellation of the Ram, or he-lamb. The Lamb, therefore, became the symbol of the young triumphant god. ... At an earlier date—owing to the precession of the equinoxes—the Sun at the spring passage stood in the constellation of the Bull; so, in the older worships of Egypt, and of Persia and of India, it was the Bull that was sacred and the symbol of god. ... In the representation of the Zodiac in the Temple of Denderah (in Egypt) the figure of Virgo is annotated by

---

[42] David Forsyth, *Psychology and Religion* London 1935, p. 97.

[43] This hypothesis is ably presented in the following works: C. F. Volney, *The Ruins, or Meditation on the Revolutions of Empires and the Law of Nature* trans. Joel Barlow (New York: Peter Eckler Press, 1890); Charles F. Dupuis, *The Origin of All Religious Worship* (New Orleans: 1872); Edward Carpenter, *Pagan and Christian Creeds: Their Origin and Meaning* (New York: Harcourt Brace and Company, 1920); Derald Massey, *Pagan Christs*; idem, *Christianity and Mythology*; Arthur Drews; *The Christ Myth* (London: T. Fisher Unwin, 1910); T. W. Doane; *Bible Myths*; Rev. Dr. Richard B. Westbrook, *The Eliminator* and his *The Bible—Whence and What* (Philadelphia: J. B. Lippincott Co., 1890).

a smaller figure of Isis with Horus in her arms; and the Roman Church fixed the celebration of Mary's assumption into the glory at the very date (15th August) of the said constellation's disappearance from sight in the blaze of the solar rays, and her birth on the date (8* Sept.) of the same constellation's reappearance. . . . Jesus himself ... is purported to have been born like the other sungods, Baccus, Apollo, Osiris, on the 25th day of December, the day of the Sun's rebirth, i.e., the first day which obviously lengthens after the 21st of December.[44]

Vegetation cults, it seems are older than stellar or solar cults, but were later blended with them. In the primitive vegetation-god sacrifice, the victim was, it is believed, originally the king, or head-man, of the tribe or clan. It was believed by ancient man that the prosperity of the tribe depended on the well-being of the ruler. If the king became old and feeble, it was considered a foregone conclusion that the nation or tribe would suffer a similar decline. So the king, who was usually regarded as a god in human form, was sacrificed, and replaced with a younger and more vigorous man. After much passage of time, the son of the king was substituted in the sacrificial rite, and being also the offspring of divinity, he was properly called the son of the god. At a still later period, a condemned criminal was chosen in the place of the royal victim. This culprit was given regal honors for a time, then put to death. He was generally slain while bound to a sacred tree, with arms outstretched in the form of a cross. After being entombed, he was believed to rise from the dead within three days; the three-day period representing the return of vegetation. The question naturally arises: Why three days? The answer is, that the three-day period is based on the three-day interval between the Old and New Moons.[45] It is still believed by certain persons

---

[44] Edward Carpenter, *Love's Coming of Age* (New York, 1926), pp. 146-149.
[45] Frazer, *Folk-Lore in the Old Testament*, p. 29.

of a superstitious type that there is an intimate connection between the phases of the moon and the growth of crops.

According to the Chaldean historian Berosus, there was a religious festival celebrated annually in ancient Babylon, known as the Sacaea. The duration of the fete was five days, and for that length of time servants and masters exchanged places in society, the servants giving orders and the masters obeying them. The king temporarily abdicated the throne, and a mock-king called Zoganes reigned in his place. But after the five days were over, the mock-king was dethroned and scourged, and then either hanged or crucified. An eminent Egyptologist has noted that:

> The victims of these human sacrifices were generally crucified, or else killed and then "hung on a tree," until the evening. In this regard it is interesting to notice that in Acts the writer mistakenly speaks of Jesus as having been slain and then hanged on a tree, as though this were a common phrase coming readily to his mind; and the word "hanged" is frequently used in Greek to denote crucifixion.[46]

Among the advocates of the non-historicity of Jesus, John M. Robertson and L. Gordon Rylands are widely known. In his *Evolution of Christianity*,[47] Mr. Rylands contends that the name Jesus is the Greek equivalent of the Hebrew Joshua. Joshua, it seems, was an ancient Hebrew sun-god, who was demoted to the status of a man by the priests of the Yahweh cult. However, the worship of Joshua was continued in secret by his devotees, until the fall of Jerusalem. After that event, secrecy was no longer necessary, so that the Joshua cult again

---

[46] Sir Arthur Weigall, *The Paganism in Our Christianity* (New York and London,
1928), pp. 77-78.
[47] L. Gordon Rylands, *The Evolution of Christianity* (London: Watts & Co.,
1927)

came out into the open. The sacrificed Jesus, or Joshua, according to Robertson and Rylands, was not a historical personage, but a character in a mystery play. "What is clear," declares Mr. Robertson,

> is that the central narrative of the gospel biography, the story of the Last Supper, The Agony, Betrayal, Trial, and Crucifixion, is neither a contemporary report nor a historical tradition, but the simple transcript of a Mystery-Drama.[48]

The views of Rylands and Robertson have been challenged by Joseph McCabe[49] and Sir Arthur Weigall. Mr. McCabe holds that it is more reasonable to conclude from the available evidence that Jesus did actually live; that he was a man who was gradually turned into a god. Sir Arthur Weigall counters the mythicists with a very ingenious theory. According to Sir Arthur, when Jesus was crucified he did not die, but only swooned; and that afterwards he was revived by his friends and spirited away. The Matthew narrator tells us that the chief priests and Pharisees requested Pilate to station a guard of Roman soldiers at the tomb of Jesus: "Lest his disciples come by night and steal him away, and say unto the people, he is risen from the dead." It is stated in the Bible account that the guard was not placed at the tomb until the second night after the burial of Jesus. Weigall suggests that Jesus was taken out of the tomb on the first night; so that the soldiers stood watch over an empty sepulcher. Since the report was abroad that Jesus had died on the cross, accounts of subsequent appearances must have convinced many persons that he had risen from the dead.

---

[48] J. M. Robertson, *A Short History of Christianity*, 2nd rev. ed. (London: Watts & Co., 1913), p. 12.
[49] McCabe, Joseph, *The Story of Religious Controversy* (Boston: The Stratford Co., Publishers, 1929)

The myths and legends concerning such pagan christs as Osiris, Horus, Adonis, Krishna, *etc.*, were later interpolated into the biography of Jesus. The famous dramatist, George Moore, in his play "The Apostle," also depicts Jesus as surviving the crucifixion. Finally Paul meets Jesus in a monastery, whence Jesus had fled into exile. When Paul discovered that Jesus had not died on the cross, and as a result had not risen from the dead, he became furious, and in a fit of temper, slew Jesus. This is a symbolic way of showing that historic Christianity is based on the teachings of St. Paul rather than on those of Jesus; that the influence of Paul triumphed over that of Jesus in the early church.

Whether Jesus lived or not, we may conclude with certainty that Christianity is of pagan origin. December the twenty-fifth is celebrated as the birthday of Jesus Christ. This date is an approximation of the Winter Solstice, and the birthday of several pagan sun-gods. Its pagan derivation is beyond all dispute. "The Gospels say nothing as to the day of Christ's birth," declares Sir James George Frazer,

> and accordingly the early Church did not celebrate it. In time, however, the Christians of Egypt came to regard the sixth of January as the date of the Nativity, and the custom of commemorating the birth of the Savior on that day gradually spread until by the fourth century it was universally established in the East. But at the end of the third or the beginning of the fourth century the Western Church, which had never recognized the sixth of January as the day of the Nativity, adopted the twenty-fifth of December as the true date, and in time its decision was accepted also by the Eastern Church.[50]

The reason why the change was made is best stated by an ancient Syrian writer, who was himself a Christian. Says he:

[50] Frazer, *The Golden Bough*, p. 358

The reason why the fathers transferred the celebration of the sixth of January to the twenty-fifth of December was this. It was a custom of the heathen to celebrate on the same twenty-fifth of December the birthday of the Sun, at which time they kindled lights in token of festivity. In these solemnities and festivities the Christians also took part. Accordingly when the doctors of the Church perceived that the Christians had a leaning to this festival, they took counsel and resolved that the true Nativity should be solemnized on that day and the festival of the Epiphany on the sixth of January. Accordingly, along with this custom, the practice had prevailed of kindling fires till the sixth.

Easter is likewise of heathen origin. It is an approximation of the Vernal Equinox. Easter falls on the first Sunday after the first full moon after the Vernal Equinox (the twenty- first of March), or as late as the twenty-fifth of April. The very name of the festival betrays its pagan source, for Easter is a variant of Eostre or Ostara, the name of the Anglo-Saxon goddess of Spring. The Festival of Sr. George takes place on April 23. It is a Christian replica of the ancient Parilia, or Birthday of Rome. St. George was originally the Egyptian god, Horus, who slew the Egyptian devil. Set, in the form of a dragon. The Festival of All Souls is a Christian copy of the ancient Egyptian Feast of the Lamps, and as Arthur Weigall observes:

> Christians unconsciously perpetuate the worship of Osiris and the commemoration of all his subjects in the Kingdom of the Dead.[51]

The mysterious doctrine of the Trinity loses the character of mystery when we consider its origin. In ancient Egypt the Sun was worshipped as a god. Since there can be no life without sunlight, the Sun was recognized as the Creator of life, and

---

[51] Weigall, *The Paganism in Our Christianity*, p. 127.

since without adequate sunlight living things wither and die, the Sun was regarded as the Protector, or preserver of life. An excess of sunlight destroys life, so that the Sun was also known as the Destroyer of life. The Sun, considered in its three aspects of Creator, Protector, and Destroyer, was indeed a Trinity in Unity. Solar and stellar symbolism have profoundly affected the Christian religion. For instance, in the Apocalypse, we read of the Four Beasts and the Four Horsemen. Taken literally the narrative does not make sense, but when we learn that the beasts are zodiacal constellations and the horsemen, planets, we get a much clearer perception of the matter. In Revelation 4:7, we read that:

> *And the first beast was like a lion, and the second beast like a calf, and the third beast had a face as a man, and the fourth beast was like a flying eagle.*

These animals were the constellations that were situated at the four cardinal points of the Zodiac five thousand years ago. They were Taurus the Bull (Vernal Equinox), Leo the Lion (Summer Solstice), Scorpio the Scorpion (Autumnal Equinox), and Aquarius the Waterman (Winter Solstice). The reader will notice that in the Bible the Eagle has been substituted for the Scorpion. According to Sir Godfrey Higgins:

> The signs of the Zodiac, with the exception of the Scorpion, which was exchanged by Dan for the Eagle, were carried by the different tribes of the Israelites on their standards; and Taurus, Leo, Aquarius, and Scorpio of the Eagle, the four signs of Reuben, Judah, Ephraim, and Dan, were placed at the four corners—the four cardinal points—of their encampment, evidently in allusion to the cardinal points of the sphere, the equinoxes and solstices.[52]

---

[52] Higgins, Anacalypsis, vol. 2, P. 105.

Now for the Horsemen and their steeds. The first horseman is a conqueror, armed with a bow and wearing a crown, and riding a white horse. (This is the planet Venus.) The second horse is red, and on it is a warrior with a sword. (The red planet is of course mars, worshipped by the ancients as the god of war.) The third horse is black (the planet Saturn), and his rider holds a pair of balances aloft. (The balances may be emblematic of the zodiacal constellation Libra, for the sun was in that constellation when day and night were equal, just as though weighed on a pair of scale pans.) The fourth horse is of a pale complexion (pale green or blue-green, the color of the planet Mercury), and astride him sits Death. (The ancient Babylonians built their temples in seven stages, each of a different color, representing the sun, the moon, and the five planets visible to the naked eye. The colors of the four horses point to their origin in the astrological lore of Babylonia.)

The sacred monogram Chi-Rho, so called because composed of the Greek letters chi (X) and rho (P), is of Egyptian origin. According to Sir Flinders Petrie, the Egyptologist, the monogram Chi-Rho was the emblem of the Egyptian god, Horus, thousands of years before Christs.

The letters *IHS* constitute another sacred monogram of Christ. These letters were also the sacred symbol of the Greek sun-god Baccus, or Dionysus. The Christians adopted them as they did many other symbols from the pagans. These letters form the root of the name Jesus. *HIS* when translated from Greek to Latin becomes *IES*. Adding the Latin masculine suffix, US, we get *IES* plus *US*, which equals *IESUS*. In English the *I* becomes *J*, hence we get JESUS.

Many incidents of the Gospel stories can be explained only as myths. We read of Satan leading Jesus to the mountain top. The devil has been represented in Jewish and Christian folklore and art in the form of a goat. We see Satan in Medieval paintings with the hooves, horns, and tail of a goat. The Greek god Pan was part goat, and is represented as leading Zeus to the mountain top. In ancient Babylon the goat was the emblem of the zodiacal constellation Capricorn. The sun reached the lowest point in the celestial sphere in this constellation, after which it began to climb toward the highest point. So the goat- god is imagined to lead the sun-god toward the highest point, figuratively called the mountain top.

In Greek mythology we read of the savior Dionysus riding upon two asses, which afterwards he had changed into celestial constellations. Jesus is pictured as riding into Jerusalem upon the two asses, i.e., upon as ass and colt, the foal of an ass.[53] In Babylonia the symbol of the zodiacal constellation Cancer, in which the sun reached the highest point of its apparent path, was the ass and foal.

The signs and constellations of the Zodiac have been referred to several times in this essay, so it is advisable that we consider their origin and meaning. The Zodiac is an imaginary band encircling the celestial sphere. It stretches eight degrees on each side of the Ecliptic, the apparent path of the sun. The Zodiac is divided into twelve equal sections, each corresponding to one month. Due to the annual revolution of the earth, the sun appears to make one complete circuit through the Zodiac in one year, staying in each sign one month. The signs of the Zodiac and the constellations of the Zodiac were originally the same, but due to the precession of the equinoxes, each sign moves westward into the next constellation in about 2155 years. A sign therefore makes a complete circuit of the heavens in about 26,000 years. We are told by Professor Harding, the noted astronomer and mathematician, that the signs and constellations of the Zodiac coincided about 300 B.C., and before that about 26,000 B.C. Since they were widely known thousands of years before 300

---

[53] Matthew 21:5-7.

B.C., they evidently originated not later than about 26,000 B.C.[54]

The constellations of the Zodiac have the following names: Aries (the Ram or Lamb), Taurus (the Bull or Ox), Gemini (the Twins), Cancer (the Crab), Leo (the Lion), Virgo (the Virgin), Libra (the Balances), Scorpio (the Scorpion), Sagittarius (the Archer), Capricornus (the Goat), Aquarius (the Water-carrier), Pisces (the Fishes). The following speculations on the origin of the names of the constellations are about as accurate as any list which might be complied, the majority of students of the subject being in general agreement upon them. The constellations of the Lamb, the Bull, and the Twins, were star groups through which the sun passed in the spring, in which time of the year occurred the seasons of sheep-raising, ploughing, and goat-breeding. The Twins were originally the two-kids, since the young of goats are frequently born two at a time. The Crab was so called because the sun reached its most northern point in that constellation, and then returned toward the south, figuratively moving backward like a crab. The Lion is the star group through which the sun moved in July, when its heat was most powerful, being compared with the most ferocious of the beasts. The Virgin is an emblem of the harvest season, when the young girls were sent out to glean in the fields. The Balance is the constellation in which the sun moved when day and night were equal in length, just as if they were weighed in a balance. The stars of the Scorpio were hidden by the sun during the season of unhealthy weather and of plagues, which were imagined to strike like a scorpion. Stars called the Archer reigned over the hunting season, when the hunter shot game with the bow and arrow. In the Goat the sun reached the lowest point in its course, after which it began to climb toward the north again, just as the wild goat climbs toward the summit of the hill. The Water-Carrier marked the position of the solar orb during the rainy season. The stars of the Fishes

---

[54] See Professor Arthur M. Harding, *Astronomy* (Garden City, NY, 1935).

constituted that group through which the sun passed when the fishing season was at its height.

Many learned Christian scholars do not believe that Jesus had any idea of starting a new religion or of establishing a church. They believe that the real founder of institutional Christianity was St. Paul. Yet we read of Jesus referring to Peter as the rock upon which the church is to be built. St. Peter is also popularly represented as the gate-keeper of heaven. The name Peter comes from the Greek word *Petra*, which means "Rock." This may be a pseudonym, since he is also referred to as Simon called Peter. That is, he may have been named Simon, and was called the Rock because of some trait of character, just as General Stonewall Jackson was so called because he stood up against the enemy like a stone wall. It is interesting to note that there was a popular Semitic god named Simon, and that the Egyptian god, *Petra*, was represented as being the door-keeper of heaven, the earth and the underworld.

In the Gospel of St. John, Jesus is presented in the office of the Judge of the Dead: "For the Father judgeth no man, but hath committed all judgment unto the Son." (John 5:22). Osiris enacted this role in the Egyptian religion. He is shown on the monuments occupying the judgment seat, and holding the staff of authority and the *crux ansata*; and on his breast is a St. Andrew's cross. His throne is designed like a chessboard, the two colors representing the good and evil which come before him for judgment. The trial of the soul before Osiris in the Hall of Judgment is described in detail in the *Book of the Dead*.[55] According to the Hindus, Krishna will occupy the judgment seat on the last day.

As the stories of slain and risen gods are traced backward into the dim and distant past, we finally come to Africa. One of the

---

[55] E. A. Wallis Budge, *The Book of the Dead, The Hieroglyphic Transcript of the Papyrus of AMI* (New Hyde Park, NY: University Books, Inc., 1960).

oldest religious celebrations of the ancient Egyptians was the Sed Festival. Sir Flinders Petrie explains it as follows:

> A special festival of the identity of the king with Osiris seems to have been celebrated every thirty years, and a greater festival of the same nature every one-hundred and twenty years. These periods are the lapse of a week and a month in the shifting calendar. The festival was called the sed or tail feast, as marking the end of a period. From the various representations, it has been gathered that at stated times the king was killed to prevent his old age impairing the fertility of the country, an African belief.[56]

The earliest religion of Egypt has been traced back to Central Africa. "The oldest structure of the people," says Petrie, was that which resembled the African in beliefs and practices. There is a large body of customs, especially those concerning the dead, which are closely alike in ancient Egypt and modern Central Africa. In this stratum, probably preceding 10,000 B.C., animal worship was usual; so strong was the primitive influence that this remained in practice down to the Roman age. The source of this was a sense of kinship of men and animals.[57]

The same high authority, Flinders Petrie, further states,

> that the religion, like the population of Egypt, was always being mixed by successive migrations of invaders. The old African ideas which underlay it all still survive in Central Africa.[58]

---

[56] Sir W. M. Flinders Petrie, *Ancient Egyptians*, vol, 11 of Herbert Spencer's *Descriptive Sociology*, p. 41.
[57] Sir W. M. Flinders Petrie, *The Gods of Ancient Egypt*, in Hammerton's Wonders of the Past (New York, 1937), p. 667.
[58] *Ibid.*, p. 678.

Limitations of both time and space prevent a more extended survey of this subject. The author hopes that some of the readers of this essay will find the time to make a critical study of Christian origins. Comparative religion is a fascinating study, and all students of human history should be well grounded in the fundamental principles of this important branch of social anthropology.